THE M...
THE V...

THE MILK OF THE WORD

An Introduction to
The Christian Faith

PETER BARNES

Minister of Nambucca River Presbyterian Church,
New South Wales

THE BANNER OF TRUTH TRUST

THE BANNER OF TRUTH TRUST
3 Murrayfield Road, Edinburgh EH12 6EL
PO Box 621, Carlisle, Pennsylvania 17013, USA

*

© Peter Barnes 1985
First published 1985
ISBN 0 85151 434 0

*

Set in 12/13pt VIP Garamond
Typeset, printed and bound in Great Britain by
Hazell Watson & Viney Limited,
Member of the BPCC Group,
Aylesbury, Bucks

Contents

Preface

'Solidity, indeed, becomes the Pen
Of him that writeth things Divine to men'.

So wrote John Bunyan. But experience of teaching the Word in a country where English was not the native language has convinced the author that simplicity is also required. Hence, this little book is sent out with the prayer that it may prove to be both solid and simple in its setting forth of biblical truths.

'Like newborn babes, long for the pure milk of the word, that by it you may grow in respect to salvation' (I Pet. 2:2).

PETER BARNES
*PO Box 87, 21 West Street,
Macksville, Australia, 2447*

1

THE WORD OF GOD

1. *How Can We Know About God?*

In 1510 a young German monk named Martin Luther visited Rome. Here he was told that if he climbed what were supposed to be Pilate's stairs on his hands and knees, repeating the Lord's Prayer at each step and kissing it for good measure, he would help deliver a soul from purgatory.[1] Luther climbed the stairs, all the time repeating the Lord's Prayer and kissing each step. But when he reached the top, he asked himself, 'Who knows whether these things please God?' Luther's question is our question too: How can we know about God?

Because God created all things (Gen. 1), all things point, in some way, back to Him. The heavens declare His glory (Ps. 19:1), although they do it without words (Ps. 19:3). In God's creation, there is clear evidence that there is a Creator (Rom. 1:20). William Paley said that the world is something like a watch, and this shows that there is a watchmaker. There are beautiful lakes and trees (see Matt. 6:28–29), but because of man's sin the creation was cursed (Gen. 3:17–18; 5:29; Rom. 8:22), so there are also hurricanes and earthquakes.

[1] The Roman Catholic Church teaches that those who die without sufficient merit suffer in purgatory before going to heaven. This is not taught in God's Word.

But a broken watch still shows that there is a watchmaker. And the beauty and order of the earth should be enough to lead all people to praise their Creator and Preserver (Gen. 8:22; Ps. 104; Matt. 5:45; Acts 14:17).

There is another way that we can know something about God. We are all created in God's image (Gen. 1:26), so we all have some idea of God within us. The Bible says that God has set eternity in our hearts (Eccles. 3:11). We all have a conscience, some idea of right and wrong. This is true even of heathen people (Rom. 2:14–16; 1 Cor. 5:1; 1 Pet. 2:12; 3:16; Luke 11:13).

Yet if we only had the testimony of creation and our consciences, we could not know much about God at all. We could only touch 'the fringes of His ways' (Job 26:14; see also vv. 8–9 and Eccles. 8:17). For example, we could know that God is our Creator, but we would not know that He is Triune. Calvin said that we would be like a traveller passing through a field on a dark night. Suddenly, lightning flashes and the traveller can see far and wide, but just as suddenly the traveller is back in darkness again, and cannot find his way.

However, God has not left us in such darkness. He has given us a book, the Bible, which is His Word. As Isaac Watts put it,

'The heavens declare Thy glory, Lord,
In every star Thy wisdom shines;

[10]

But when our eyes behold Thy Word,
We read Thy Name in fairer lines.'

The Bible actually consists of sixty-six books, written originally in the Hebrew, Aramaic or Greek languages over a period of about 1,600 years. Its writers included kings (David and Solomon), fishermen (Peter and John), a herdsman (Amos), a tax-collector (Matthew) and many others. All in all, God used about forty different men to give us His Word. So if we wish to know about God, we must read and hear His Word, the Bible. This alone is God's Word – we can add nothing to it, neither can we take anything from it (Deut. 4:2; 12:32; Prov. 30:5–6; Rev. 22:18–19). The Lord Jesus Himself condemned the Pharisees for daring to add to God's Word (Mark 7:1–13). This does not mean that the Bible reveals everything that could be known about God and His ways (Deut. 29:29; John 21:25; 1 Cor. 13:12). For example, God has not told us the date of Jesus' second coming (Acts 1:7). But it does mean that the Bible is sufficient and completely true, and reading it, as we must, with reverence and understanding, we can know that God is speaking through it to us.

2. *Men Spoke from God*

The Bible is God's book but God caused it to be written by men. Peter said that 'men moved by the Holy Spirit spoke from God' (2 Pet. 1:21). Each book of the Bible has two authors – the Holy Spirit, who is the divine author, and the prophet or the apostle who is the human author. We should not be afraid to recognize that the Bible is human as well as divine. There are many places in the New Testament where the human author of an Old Testament passage is named (e.g. Matt. 2:17–18; 3:3; 4:14–16; Mark 7:10; 12:19,36; Acts 1:16–17; Rom. 9:27–28; 10:19–20).

The human side of the Bible can be seen in many other ways. The authors have different styles of writing. Isaiah's style is majestic, whereas that of Amos is harsh. In the New Testament, Luke and Acts are written in very good Greek, while Mark and 2 Peter are rather rough. The Holy Spirit did not inspire men in a mechanical way, but worked through their different gifts and abilities. Luke even says that he did some research before he wrote his Gospel (Luke 1:3).

If we read carefully, we shall find traces of the human hand in Scripture. In the original Greek, Romans 8:12–13 is an unfinished sentence, although it is clear that Paul meant to go on to say that Christians are debtors to the Spirit. Another untidy passage can be found in 1 Cor. 1:14–16. Here, Paul recalls the names of the people he had baptized, but in v.16 he suddenly remembers that he had also baptized Stephanas' household. He even adds, 'I do not know whether I baptized any other.' Daniel confesses that he did not understand all that he had written (Dan. 12:8–9), while Peter confesses that

THE WORD OF GOD

some of Paul's writings were hard to understand (2 Pet. 3:16).

The Bible is fully human, yet without error, as Christ Jesus is fully human, yet without sin. The Bible, however, records the sins and errors of man. Noah's drunkenness in Gen. 9:20–21 is there to warn us to stand firm against sin. Similarly, not all that Job's three friends taught is to be received as God's truth for in Job 42:7 God says that they were not completely correct in all that they had said.[2]

So we should recognize that the Bible is a human book. God could have spoken through the human authors in such a way that nothing human would have been left in their writings – after all, He spoke through Balaam's donkey (Num. 22) – but He did not choose to work in this way. It has been said that we can hear the recorded voice of the singer and also the scratches on the record. This is true, but the scratches on the record do not mean that the singer misses any notes.

3. The Old Testament as God's Word

Many people today, including some who call themselves Christians, say that they believe in the New Testament, or parts of it, but not in the Old Testament. They often say that the God of the Old Testament is an angry God who punishes people but the God of the New Testament is loving and merciful. Perhaps these people have never read Hosea 11:8–9 or

[2] 1 Cor. 3:19 still cites Job 5:13 as a part of God's truth.

Luke 16:19–31. Whoever rejects the Old Testament must also reject the New Testament, for the two Testaments fit perfectly together. As Augustine said, 'The New Testament is concealed in the Old; the Old Testament is revealed in the New.' Jesus says that if we do not believe Moses, we will not believe Him (John 5:46–47).

Some scholars have taught that God inspired the prophets and the apostles, but not their words. The truth is that God inspired both the men (2 Pet. 1:21) and their words (2 Tim. 3:16). But in the Bible the emphasis is always on the Word as God's Word rather than upon the men as God's men. God told Joshua, 'This book of the law shall not depart from your mouth, but you shall meditate on it day and night, so that you may be careful to do according to all that is written in it' (Josh. 1:8). God took great care to see that His Word was written down accurately so that it could be handed down from one generation to the next (look up Ex. 24:4; Deut. 17:18; 31:9,24–29; Josh. 24:26; 1 Sam. 10:25; Isa. 8:16; 30:8; Jer. 36:4; 45:1; Dan. 9:2; Hab. 2:2; also Col. 4:16; 1 Thess. 5:27; Rev. 1:3). Because of this, people did not have to guess what God might have said; they could read God's Word for themselves or have it read to them (look up Ex. 24:7; Deut. 31:11; Josh. 8:34–35; 2 Kings 22:8–16; Neh. 8:8; 9:3; 13:1).

God's Word in the Old Testament is perfect and true (Ps. 19:7; 119:89,142,160). But we must come to a right understanding of it, for some of its laws were only for the Old Testament period. Examples of these laws include circumcision (Gen. 17:10–14; see Gal. 5:2–4), the food laws (Lev. 11; see Mark 7:19; Acts 10:9–15; 1 Tim. 4:1–5) and the sacrifices (e.g. Lev. 16; see Heb. 10:1–18). God gave these laws, but only for a time, until the Messiah came and a new age began.

When the prophets spoke in the Old Testament, they spoke God's Word; they did not just give out their own religious views. The phrase 'Thus says the Lord' occurs about 2,000 times in the Old Testament. The prophets used this phrase to tell the people that the Word of the prophet is also the Word of God (see Jer. 36:8, 10).[3]

When God called Jeremiah to be His prophet, He put His words in Jeremiah's mouth (Jer. 1:9). We find this same thought in many places in the Old Testament (e.g. Isa. 51:16; 59:21; Ezek. 3:1–4). In Amos 3:7–8 we read, 'Surely the Lord God does nothing unless He reveals His secret counsel to His servants the prophets. A lion has roared! Who will not fear? The Lord God has spoken! Who can but prophesy?' (see also Num. 12:6–8). The Old Testament is God's Word, and this is truth (2 Sam. 7:28). Therefore, the worst thing that happened to Israel occurred when God withdrew His Word from His people (Amos 8:11–12).

False prophets, then as today, spoke from their own imaginations (Jer. 14:14; 23:16; Ezek. 13:3),

[3] Occasionally, a false prophet used the phrase (e.g. Jer. 28:2).

but the true prophet waited for God to speak first (Deut. 18:20; Jer. 9:12; 23:21–22). Only then did the prophet cry, 'O land, land, land, hear the Word of the Lord!' (Jer. 22:29).

4. *Christ's View of the Bible*

In the twentieth century many theologians have spoken strongly against the teaching that the Bible is wholly true and contains no errors. Emil Brunner thought that such an idea made the Bible into an idol, Paul Tillich felt that it was demonic, while Archbishop William Temple claimed that those who believe in a Bible without error lack spirituality. If we wish to be Christians, however, we should hear first what the Lord Jesus teaches about the Bible. In John 10:35 our Lord says that 'the Scripture cannot be broken', and in John 17:17 He says in His prayer to the Father, 'Thy Word is truth'. These two statements show that Jesus' view of the Bible is very different from that of many churchmen today.

When Jesus was tempted by the devil, He wielded the sword of the Spirit which is God's Word. Three times Jesus quoted from the book of Deuteronomy, saying, 'It is written' (Matt. 4:4,7,10). To Jesus, 'It is written' means 'It is therefore true'. When the Sadducees denied the resurrection of the body, our Lord accused them of not understanding the Scriptures or the power of God (Matt. 22:29). Similarly, in His debate with the Pharisees over whether men's traditions should be obeyed, Jesus stated that what

Moses said (Mark 7:10) was also what God said (Matt. 15:4). Even the smallest letter or stroke in God's Word is important (Matt. 5:17–19).

Because the Scripture comes from God, Jesus was certain that its prophecies had to be fulfilled (see Matt. 26:24; Mark 9:12; 12:10–11; 14:27; Luke 22:37; John 13:18). In fact, Jesus declared that 'it is easier for heaven and earth to pass away than for one stroke of a letter of the law to fail' (Luke 16:17). Even when Jesus appeared to speak contrary to Moses' law on divorce, He did so by appealing to the original meaning of the law as given in Genesis (see Matt. 19:1–9).

Our Lord testified to the truth of many parts of the Old Testament that are often regarded as myths. He referred to Adam and Eve (Matt. 19:4–5), Sodom (Luke 17:28–30), Noah (Matt. 24:37–39), Jonah being swallowed by a fish (Matt. 12:39–41), and Lot's wife being turned into a pillar of salt (Luke 17:31–32).

Jesus also looked forward to the time when the Holy Spirit would come to the apostles and inspire them as they wrote the New Testament (John 14:26; 16:12–13). Jesus obviously intended that the record of His work and teaching would be preserved for all time (Matt. 24:35; 26:13; John 17:20).

In the nineteenth century, an Anglican bishop, Charles Gore, admitted that Jesus taught that the Old Testament was completely true, but added that Jesus was wrong in teaching this. We live in strange times. People want to be Christians without following Christ, which is rather like expecting crops to grow without planting anything in the first place. How different is the Bible's teaching! God tells us, 'To this one I will look, to him who is humble and contrite of spirit, and who trembles at My word' (Isa. 66:2). A Christian will follow Christ in all things, including His view of the Bible.

5. *The New Testament as God's Word*

The teaching of the whole Bible concerning its own authority is summed up in 2 Timothy 3:16. Here, Paul says that 'All Scripture is inspired by God'. B. B. Warfield, the American Presbyterian scholar who died in 1921, tells us that the wording in the Greek is even stronger. It should be 'All Scripture is God-breathed', as the New International Version has it. God did not just breathe into the Scripture, but Scripture was, in fact, breathed out by Him. It is 'ex-pired' rather than in-spired.

We have seen that the Old Testament writers gave us God's Word. The New Testament writers support this claim (see Acts 24:14). In many places, the New Testament quotes the Old Testament, saying that the author was God Himself. Examples of this are found in Acts 13:34–35 (citing Isa. 55:3 and Ps. 16:10) and Hebrews 5:5–6 (Ps. 2:7; 110:4). Old Testament passages are also attributed to Christ (Heb. 2:10–12 citing Ps. 22:22; Heb. 10:5–7 citing Ps. 40:6–8) and the Holy Spirit (Heb. 3:7–11 citing Ps. 95:7–11; see 'the Spirit of Christ' in 1 Pet. 1:10–11). So the Old Testament comes from God, the Triune God.

The New Testament writers also taught that they too were recording the Word of God. The apostles were the Lord's men chosen for special purposes. They were:

(a) witnesses of Christ, especially after His resurrection (Acts 1:21–22; 1 Cor. 9:1);

(b) directly commissioned by the Lord Jesus (Gal. 1:1);

(c) given special powers by God (Rom. 15:18–19; 2 Cor. 12:12).

Therefore God moved some of the apostles to write the New Testament, or, as in the case of Mark and Luke, men authorized by the apostles.

As a man thus commissioned by the Lord, Paul could say that his words came from the Holy Spirit (1 Cor. 2:13) and so were to be obeyed as the Lord's commandment (1 Cor. 14:37). He was certain that not even an angel from heaven could teach a different gospel (Gal. 1:6–9). Paul did not issue commands on every subject (see Rom. 14:5–6; 1 Cor. 7:8–9), but when he was moved to give commands, he did so in the name of the Lord Jesus (2 Thess. 3:6,12). Paul knew that his message was not the word of man but the Word of God (1 Thess. 2:13). The apostle Peter also put Paul's letters with 'the rest of the Scriptures', which shows that he regarded them as part of God's Word (2 Pet. 3:15–16).

The two Testaments form one unified book. Both testify that the Word of the Lord abides for ever (1 Pet. 1:24–25; Isa. 40:6–8). 1 Timothy 5:18 cites Deuteronomy 25:4 and Luke 10:7, and treats them both as Scripture. The book of Revelation calls itself a book of prophecy, just like the Old Testament books (Rev. 1:3).

Lastly, Paul could even write 'the Scripture says to Pharaoh' when it would have been more natural to have written 'God says to Pharaoh' (Rom. 9:17; see also Gal. 3:8). It is no wonder that Augustine thought he heard God cry out, 'Man, O man, what my Scripture says, I say.' The Bible claims to be God's very Word, complete and without error when it was first given. By now we should be able to see why B. B. Warfield said that to try to explain away the Scripture's testimony to its own full authority was like trying to avoid an avalanche.

Many years ago, the great Augustine wrote fifteen books on the Trinity. He finished with this prayer: 'O Lord, one God, the Triune God, whatsoever I have said in these Books that comes of Thy prompting, may Thy people acknowledge it: for what I have said that comes only of myself, I ask of Thee and of Thy people pardon.' This prayer is very humble and very Christian, for Augustine was not an apostle. The apostles, however, did not finish their books with prayers like this, for they knew they were writing God's Word. That also was very humble and very Christian.

6. *Conclusions*

We began our study with Luther's question: 'How can we know about God?' We can now answer that question. We can know about God through His Word, the Bible. This does not mean that if you own a Bible and read it, you will automatically go to heaven. We need the Holy Spirit to open our eyes before we can understand what God is saying to us (1 Cor. 2:14). That is why Charles Wesley wrote:

> 'Come, Holy Ghost, for moved by Thee
> The prophets wrote and spoke;
> Unlock the truth, Thyself the key;
> Unseal the sacred book.'

To know God, we need God's Word and God's Spirit.

Sometimes you might hear someone say that the Bible is true when it teaches doctrine and ethics, but on other questions it might well be wrong. We must be careful here. When David said, 'The trees of the forest will sing for joy before the Lord' (1 Chron. 16:33), he was not teaching anything about science. Even when the Bible says that 'the sun rises and the sun sets' (Eccles. 1:5), it is only speaking of the sun as it appears to us. We still speak in the same way today even though we know that the sun does not actually rise or set. However, when the Bible tells of the creation of the universe and of Adam and Eve in Genesis 1–2, it is not speaking poetically. In this case, we cannot say that it is 'spiritually true' but 'scientifically false'.

There are some things about the Bible that still puzzle us. Did Jesus cleanse the Temple at the beginning of His ministry (John 2:13–17) or near the end (Matt. 21:12–13)? This problem can be solved, for Christ must have cleansed the temple twice. Did Mark write Mark 16:9–20 or were these verses added later? This problem is not so easy to solve. Nevertheless, while problems like these should be studied, they must not keep us from the main reason for reading the Bible, which is to know God.

Here is some advice from Scripture which may help you in your Bible study:

(a) Read the Word. That is how the Ethiopian was led to salvation (Acts 8:28). If a man claimed to love his wife but did not bother to read her letters when she was absent from him, we would not think much of his profession. The same is true in regard to God's letter to us.

(b) Work hard at understanding the Bible (2 Tim. 2:15). Compare Scripture with Scripture and pray for understanding.

(c) Memorize passages (Ps. 119:11; Prov. 22:17–18). When Jesus was tempted, He did not reply to Satan with some vague reference to Scripture but with passages He knew by heart (Matt. 4:1–11). A good translation will help you here (*The Good News Bible* is *not* a good translation).

(d) Meditate on the Word (Ps. 1:2; 119:97) Arthur Pink used to write out a verse in the morning and consult it during the day. This helped him to draw out more truths from God's Word.

(e) Test all things according to the light of God's truth (Acts 17:11; 1 John 4:1).

(f) Apply the Word. It is meant to teach, rebuke, correct and train us (2 Tim. 3:16).

(g) Most importantly, seek Christ Jesus in all the Scriptures (see Luke 24:25–27,44; John 5:39; Acts 8:35; 2 Tim. 3:15). As we seek Him, our daily Bible study will be a delight to our souls (Jer. 15:16).

In 1747 David Brainerd, the devoted missionary to the North American Indians, lay dying. As he drew near to eternity, he spoke of the Bible: 'O that dear book – that lovely book! I shall soon see it opened! The mysteries that are in it, and the mysteries of God's providence, will be all unfolded!' Only if we nourish our souls on God's Word can we expect to have faith like that of Brainerd.

> 'Lord, Thy Word abideth,
> And our footsteps guideth;
> Who its truth believeth
> Light and joy receiveth.
>
> O that we, discerning
> Its most holy learning,
> Lord, may love and fear Thee,
> Evermore be near Thee!'
> (Henry W. Baker)

FOR FURTHER READING:

Thy Word is Truth, E. J. Young (Banner of Truth 1963)

God Has Spoken, J. I. Packer (Hodder & Stoughton 1979)

Christ and the Bible, J. W. Wenham (Tyndale Press 1972)

2

THE TRIUNE GOD

1. *What is God Like?*

Ever since the time of Adam and Eve, men have tried to find out what God is like. Some have worshipped carved idols, others have tried to contact spirits, while yet others have thought that God and the world are really the same. However, if we wish to know God, we must turn to the Bible which is God's Word, God's message to us. Nature can tell us some things about our Creator (Rom. 1:20), and so can our conscience (Rom. 2:14–16), but the Bible alone is wholly true and reliable. The Lord Jesus Himself teaches that we must be governed only by God's Word, never by human traditions about God. See Matthew 15:1–14.

In the Bible, God tells us that He is the only true God (Deut. 6:4; 1 Kings 8:60; John 17:3; James 2:19) who created the whole universe (Gen. 1:1; Isa. 40:25–26). God also tells us that He is spirit (John 4:24), which means that He does not have a body as we do. That is why we are not allowed to make pictures of Him (Ex. 20:4).

God is perfect, without any sin (Matt. 5:48), eternal, without beginning or ending (Ex. 3:14; Ps. 90:2; Isa. 40:28), everywhere at the same time (1 Kings 8:27; Ps. 139; Jer. 23:24), and able to do whatever He wishes (Ps. 115:3; 135:6; Dan. 4:35). He knows all things (1 Sam. 16:7; Ps. 147:4; Jer. 17:10), and everything, even evil and suffering, takes place according to His will (Rom. 8:28; Eph. 1:11). We sin every day – our very nature is full of sin – but God is holy (Isa. 6:3; Ps. 99:3) righteous (Ps. 145:17; Ezra 9:15; John 17:25; Rom. 2:7), good (Ps. 145:9; Mark 10:18; Acts 14:17), wise (Ps. 104:24; Rom. 11:33–36), true (Num. 23:19; Ps. 96:5; Rom. 3:4; Heb. 6:18) and full of love (Ps. 51:1; 1 John 4:8, 16). By nature, we are attracted to sin (Gen. 6:5; Eph. 2:3), but because God is holy, He hates sin (Ex. 34:7; Ps. 5:5–6; Habakkuk 1:13). Yet God can be known by man in a personal way. God's Word tells us that the Lord spoke to Moses face to face, as a man speaks with his friend (Ex. 33:11; cf. James 2:23).

God does not change. He himself has said, 'I am the Lord, I change not' (Mal. 3:6, see also James 1:17). This means that the God who has revealed Himself in the Bible is just the same today. The God who spoke to Abraham, Moses, David and Isaiah, and who sent His eternal Son, Jesus Christ, to earth, is the same now as He was before He created the heavens and the earth. If we keep this in mind, it will greatly help us as we seek after God and pray to Him.

2. *What is the Trinity?*

When Christians speak of God, they will often speak of the Trinity – Father, Son and Holy Spirit. You will not find the words 'Trinity' or 'Triune' in the Scriptures, but you will find the teaching that

God is one, yet three. Although it does not use these words, the Bible teaches that God is three Persons in the one essence (or substance). This sounds very difficult, and we must admit that no-one can understand it completely, but we can grasp something of it if we keep very closely to the Bible.

We must be very careful to avoid four common mistakes:

(a) Sometimes people have spoken as if there were three Gods, but this is a very serious error. There is only one God. Look up Deuteronomy 6:4; Isaiah 44:6; Mark 12:29,32; and 1 Corinthians 8:4.

(b) Some treat the Father as if He were the one true God, and the Son and the Spirit as if they were not really God at all. The modern sect calling themselves Jehovah's Witnesses and many modern theologians make this tragic mistake. Look up Matthew 28:19; Colossians 2:9; and Matthew 12:31–32.

(c) Some have thought of the three Persons in the Godhead as being only one Person who appears in three different forms, just as water can appear as ice or steam. However, the three Persons are distinct from one another. The Father was not crucified and the Son was not poured out on men and women on the Day of Pentecost. Look up Matthew 3:16–17; 27:46; Luke 23:46; and Acts 2:1–4,17.

(d) Sometimes you may see illustrations which are supposed to help you to understand the Trinity. For example you might see a circle divided into three parts. Each part is supposed to represent one Person of the Holy Trinity. This may appear to be helpful, but it will give you a wrong idea of God. The circle has three parts, and if you remove one part, it is no longer a circle. However, this cannot be true of the Trinity because the Father, Son and Holy Spirit are not each one-third of the Godhead. Each is fully God – but there are not three Gods! Look up the references under (b).

So you see that we can never understand God completely – only the Triune God can understand Himself (look up Matthew 11:27 and 1 Corinthians 2:11). But we can understand that He is one God in three Persons.

3. *What does the Old Testament teach about the Trinity?*
Although the main teaching about God as Trinity comes from the New Testament, God nevertheless prepared the way for this teaching by giving His people hints of it in the Old Testament. We can find these hints in many places:

(a) Sometimes God speaks of Himself in the plural. For example, in Genesis 1:26 He says, 'Let us make man in our image'. You would expect God to have said, 'I will make man in my image', but that is what He did not say. Every word of Scripture is precious (Matt. 4:4; 5:18), so there must have been a reason for God to have spoken in the plural. We now know that God was preparing His people for the time when He would reveal more clearly that

He is one God in three Persons. There are other passages where God speaks in the plural, for example Genesis 3:22; 11:5–7; and Isaiah 6:8.

(b) In Old Testament times, God often spoke to His people through an angel called 'the Angel of the Lord' ('the Angel of Jehovah'). Yet in many places the Angel of the Lord is also called 'the Lord'. In Genesis 16, for example, we read of Hagar running away from Sarai. In verse 7 the Angel of the Lord finds her and begins to speak to her. At the end of his speech, however, Hagar says that she had actually seen God (v. 13). The Angel of the Lord was undoubtedly the Lord Jesus. We can see this in other passages too – Genesis 18:1–33; Exodus 3:2,6,14; and Judges 6:11–16; 13:3,9,22.

(c) There are other places also where it is indicated that there is more than one Person in the Godhead. Just before the Israelites attacked Jericho, Joshua saw a man who is described as the commander of the Lord's army (Josh. 5:13,15). But the man (5:13) is also described as Jehovah Himself (6:2). Much later, Isaiah described the coming Messiah as both 'a child' and 'the Mighty God' (Isa. 9:6). Other passages which ought to be studied are Psalm 45:6–7; 110:1; Isaiah 48:16; Jeremiah 23:5–6; Daniel 3:25; and Hosea 1:7. If we look carefully in the Old Testament, we can see how wonderfully God was preparing His people to receive the truth about the Trinity. In fact, one of the Hebrew words for 'God' is 'Elohim', and it can be singular or plural.

4. *The Father is God*

This section will be very short because even the heretical cults agree that the Father is God. Their mistake is to think that only the Father is God.

In the Lord's Prayer, Jesus taught Christians to pray 'Our Father who art in heaven . . .' (Matt. 6:9). Later Jesus promised that the Father would give the Holy Spirit to those who ask Him (Luke 11:13). Jesus described the Temple in Jerusalem as 'my Father's house' (Luke 2:49; John 2:16). Jesus also declared that He was the Son of Man on whom God the Father had set His seal (John 6:27). In the high-priestly prayer in John Chapter 17, Jesus looked towards heaven and called upon the Father, describing Him as 'the only true God' (verses 1–3). On the cross, Jesus' last words were 'Father, into thy hands I commit my spirit.' (Luke 23:46). You will find that in the New Testament the Father is referred to as God over 250 times.

The Father is God, the first Person of the Holy Trinity. When we pray, we normally pray to Him. Only occasionally in Scripture do we read of prayers to Christ (e.g. Acts 7:59) or the Holy Spirit (e.g. Ezekiel 37:9. 'Breath' also means 'Spirit').

It is important that we understand the difference between an earthly father and God the Father. An earthly father only *becomes* a father when a child is born to him. But God never became a Father. He was always God the Father, because God the Son was always His Son.

5. *The Son is God*

When the apostle Thomas saw that the Lord Jesus had actually risen from the dead, he cried out, 'My Lord and my God.' (John 20:28). That was a very strange thing for a Jew to say. To say that a man is God is either blasphemy or high truth itself. The high priest, Caiaphas, thought it was blasphemy (Matt. 26:63–66), but Jesus praised Thomas' confession as a true one (John 20:29). Indeed, the Scriptures often declare that Jesus Christ is God (John 1:1,18; Rom. 9:5; Phil. 2:6; Tit. 2:13; Heb. 1:8; 2 Pet. 1:1; 1 John 5:20). We rightly think of Jesus as the Son of God, but this does not mean there was a time when He did not exist. Jesus is the eternal Son of God, equal to the Father (John 5:18).

Christ is exactly like the Father; He is 'the image of the invisible God' (Col. 1:15). We find this taught in the following verses:

(a) God is eternal; so is Christ (John 8:58; Rev. 1:8,17; 22:13).

(b) God is everywhere at the same time; so is Christ. This means He is with all Christians at all times (Matt. 18:20; 28:20).

(c) God does not change; neither does Christ. He is the same yesterday, today and for ever (Heb. 13:8).

(d) God knows all things; so does Christ. He even knows our hearts (John 2:24–25; Rev. 2:23).

(e) God is able to do all things; so is Christ (Phil. 3:21; Heb. 1:3).

We also find that Christ does things that only God can do:

(a) He created the world (John 1:3; Col. 1:16; Heb. 1:2–3, 10).

(b) He forgives sin in a way that no mere man could do. We can forgive sins against ourselves, but Christ forgives sins against God (Mark 2:1–12).

(c) He will judge the world at the last day (Matt. 25:32; John 5:28–29; 2 Cor. 5:10).

(d) He gives eternal life (John 10:28).

Furthermore, there are many passages in the Old Testament which speak of God, and yet when these passages are quoted in the New Testament, they are applied to the Lord Jesus. For example:

(a) When Isaiah saw the glory of God, he actually saw the Lord Jesus (Isa. 6 and John 12:39–41).

(b) When the Bible says that God created the world, it also means that Christ created all things (Ps. 102:24–27 and Heb. 1:10–12).

(c) Christians call on Christ for salvation just as the Old Testament saints called on God for salvation (Joel 2:32 and Acts 2:21; Rom. 10:13).

(d) God is the chief cornerstone, a stone of stumbling and a rock of offence – and so is Christ (Isa. 8:14; 28:16 and Rom. 9:33; 1 Pet. 2:6,8).

All this means that we should worship and praise Christ just as we do God the Father (Heb. 1:6; Rev. 5:12). The Pharisees could not understand how Christ could be David's Lord as well as his son (Matt.

22:41–46; Ps. 110:1), but if you belong to Christ, you will know.

6. *The Holy Spirit is God*

Because many of the cults and many modern theologians think that the Holy Spirit is only a force or a power and not a Person, we must first show that He is a Person before showing that He is God.

Some people get confused because the New Testament was written in Greek, and the Greek word for 'spirit' is *pneuma*, which is neuter. In English, all males are masculine, all females are feminine, and everything else is neuter. However, other languages do not work like this. In French, for example, 'the Word' is feminine in John 1:1,14. But this does not mean that Frenchmen think of Christ as a woman. It is the same with Greek. In fact, in John 16:13–14, the Holy Spirit is referred to as 'He', not 'It', even though this is not correct grammar. This shows that the Bible regards the Holy Spirit as a Person.

We can see this in other passages – the Holy Spirit teaches (Luke 12:12; John 14:26), testifies (John 15:26), guides and speaks (John 16:13, sends (Acts 13:4) and forbids (Acts 16:6–7). We can lie to Him (Acts 5:3), tempt Him (Acts 5:9), grieve Him (Eph. 4:30) and even blaspheme Him (Matt. 12:31). All these things can only be true if the Spirit is a Person.

In addition, there are many passages which show clearly that the Holy Spirit is God:

(a) A lie to the Holy Spirit is the same as a lie to God (Acts 5:3–4).

(b) The Spirit raises the dead (Rom. 8:11).

(c) He knows all things; He knows 'the depths of God' (Isa. 40:13–14; 1 Cor. 2:10–11), for He Himself is a divine Person.

(d) He is everywhere at the same time (Ps. 139:7–10). Because of this, He is able to be with all Christians at the same time (1 Cor. 3:16; 6:19).

(e) He is eternal (Hebrews 9:14).

(f) He created the world (Gen. 1:2; Ps. 104:30).

The Father is God, the Son is God, the Spirit is God – yet there is only one God. No wonder the apostle Paul asked, 'Who has known the mind of the Lord?' (Rom. 11:34). Augustine (AD 354–430) used to say, 'If you are able to comprehend Him, He is not God.' We cannot understand ourselves, let alone God (Jer. 17:9), but we can still know 'God in three Persons, blessed Trinity'.

7. *Conclusion*

There are many places in the New Testament where the three Persons in the Trinity are seen to act together. Look up Matthew 3:16–17; 28:19; 1 Corinthians 12:4–6; 2 Corinthians 13:14; Galatians 4:6; and 1 Peter 1:2.

Perhaps the best text to quote is Matthew 28:19. When the Lord Jesus was about to leave His disciples and return to His Father in heaven, He left them with some final instructions. One of these was to baptize believers in the Name of the Father and of the Son and of the Holy Spirit. Three Persons are mentioned here, but Jesus only spoke of one Name, to show that the Three are One. Back in the fourth century, a Christian writer named Gregory of Nazianzus wrote of the Trinity, saying, 'I cannot think of the One without quickly being encircled by the splendour of the Three; nor can I discern the Three without being straightway carried back to the One.'

Let us close our study with praise to the Trinity in the words of an ancient hymn:

> 'Laud and honour to the Father,
>   Laud and honour to the Son,
> Laud and honour to the Spirit,
>   Ever Three and ever One,
>   One in might, and One in glory,
>   While unending ages run.'

FOR FURTHER READING:

God Transcendent, J. G. Machen (Banner of Truth 1982)

The Three Are One, Stuart Olyott (Evangelical Press 1982)

3

JESUS CHRIST: GOD AND MAN

1. *Who is Jesus Christ?*

Early one evening Jesus called His disciples to sail across the Sea of Galilee. As their boat made its way across the water, a furious storm blew up. The disciples became very frightened and called on Jesus to do something. Jesus simply spoke, 'Peace, be still' (Mark 4:39), and at once the wind died down and all was calm again. Yet the disciples were still very frightened – of Jesus, not of the storm. They began to ask each other, 'Who is this, that even the wind and sea obey Him?' (Mark 4:41). On another occasion, Jesus asked His disciples, 'Who do you say I am?' (Mark 8:29). Later, He challenged the Pharisees, 'What do you think about the Christ? Whose son is He?' (Matt. 22:42). These questions all demand an answer, for Christ Jesus is the foundation of the Christian faith (1 Cor. 3:11). As John Newton put it,

> ' "What think ye of Christ?" is the test
> To try both your state and your scheme;
> You cannot be right in the rest,
> Unless you think rightly of Him.'

Over the centuries, there have been many answers given to the question: 'Who is Jesus Christ?' (see John 7:43). The four chief ones are:

(a) Christ is God, but not man. People called Docetists believed that Christ was divine, but that He only pretended to be a man. They thought that the divine Christ did not really suffer on the cross because God cannot suffer. The apostle John, however, says that this teaching comes from the spirit of antichrist (1 John 4:2–3; 2 John 7).

(b) Christ is the greatest of the angels. In the fourth century a man called Arius taught this, but the Church declared that his teaching was heresy. Arius used to say of Christ, 'There was [a time] when He was not.' By this, Arius meant that in the beginning only the Father existed, not the Son. Today the Jehovah's Witnesses teach this same error. However, Jesus said, 'Before Abraham was, I am.' (John 8:58). If Arius and the Jehovah's Witnesses were correct, Jesus would have said, 'Before Abraham was, I *was*.' But Jesus did not say this, because He wanted to make it very clear that He had no beginning. The Lord Jesus is eternal; He was never created.

(c) Christ is only a great man. The modern Anglican theologian, Dr John Robinson, has declared that Jesus was 'totally and utterly a man – and had never been anything other than a man or more than a man'. On this view, the wise men who came to worship the baby Jesus were really very foolish men (Matt. 2:1–12; note v.11). But Jesus never taught that He was simply a great man; He taught that He was One who had come down from heaven (John 3:31; 6:38,41).

(d) Christ is both God and Man. In the year 451 the Council of Chalcedon declared that our Lord Jesus Christ is 'perfect in Godhead' and 'perfect in manhood'. He is 'truly God and truly man'. He has two natures, divine and human, and these are joined 'without confusion, without change, without division, without separation'. *The Westminster Confession of Faith*, drawn up between 1643 and 1647, also describes the Lord Jesus as 'very God, and very man, yet one Christ, the only Mediator between God and man.' This is, in fact, what the Bible teaches. The Word (Christ) was with God and was God (John 1:1), but for us men, and for our salvation, He came down from heaven, and was incarnate by the Holy Ghost of the Virgin Mary, and was made man (Matt. 1:18–25; John 1:14).

We should not think of Christ as a divine soul in a human body, for He had, and still has, a human soul. Nor should we think that the divine Christ ceased to be God when He became a man, for even as a little child in Mary's womb He remained the eternal Son of God. Although we cannot understand completely how the two natures are joined, we must grasp that Christ is truly and fully God, and truly and fully man. Both Testaments in the Bible teach that there are two natures in the one Person. Isaiah 9:6 predicts that the Messiah would be born as a little child and yet be called 'the Mighty God' (see

Isa. 10:21). Eight hundred years later, the apostle Paul saw the fulfilment of this prophecy, and so wrote that 'in Christ all the fulness of the Deity lives in bodily form' (Col. 2:9). That is why Christians confess Christ Jesus as the God-Man.

2. *'My Lord and my God!'*

In section 4 of 'The Triune God', we saw that God's Word teaches that the Lord Jesus Christ is God. Now we will look further at the deity of Christ. Our Lord was meek and lowly in heart (Matt. 11:29), but He made the most amazing claims for Himself. He openly said, 'I and the Father are one.' (John 10:30). Later, He told Philip that 'Anyone who has seen me has seen the Father' (John 14:9). This is true because the Son is in the Father and the Father is in the Son (John 14:10).

Jesus never thought of Himself as a sinner. He said that He always did whatever pleased His Father (John 8:29), and challenged His enemies to prove Him guilty of any sin (John 8:46). Satan had no power over Him (John 14:30), for He always kept His Father's commandments (John 15:10). Truly, no man ever spoke like this man! (John 7:46). The apostles, too, were unable to find any traces of sin in the Lord Jesus (see 2 Cor. 5:21; Heb. 4:15; 7:26; 9:14; 1 Pet. 2:22; 1 John 3:5). Yet the apostles were very much aware of their own sins. When Peter met Jesus, he cried out, 'Depart from me; for I am a sinful man, O Lord' (Luke 5:8). The apostle Paul also lamented the fact that, although he hated sin, he still kept on sinning (Rom. 7:14–25).

With men, it is only those who are spiritually dead who think that they have perfectly kept God's commandments (Mark 10:20; Luke 18:9–14). It is strange, but Christians have found they are closest to God when they are most aware of the evil in their own hearts (Gen. 18:27; 32:10; Isa. 6:5). That is why so great a Christian as John Bunyan called the story of his life *Grace Abounding to the Chief of Sinners* (see 1 Tim. 1:15–16). Perhaps no-one has put this truth better than John Henry Newman: 'When a man discerns in himself most sin and humbles himself most, when his comeliness seems to him to vanish away and all his graces to wither, when he feels disgust at himself, and revolts at the thought of himself – seems to himself all dust and ashes, all foulness and odiousness – then it is that he is really rising in the Kingdom of God.' This has been true in the experience of every Christian, but it was not true of our Lord, for He knew no sin.

Furthermore, Jesus taught in a way that no other man ever taught. The Old Testament prophets used to proclaim, 'Thus says the Lord' (e.g. Haggai 1:2,7; 2:6,11). But Jesus spoke in His own name, saying, 'But I say unto you' (Matt. 5:22,28,32,34,39,44). The Gospels record that Jesus would say, 'Verily (Truly), I say unto you' (49 times; see Matt. 5:18,26; 6:2,5,16; 8:10), or 'Truly, truly, I say unto you' (25 times; see, e.g., John 1:51; 3:3). Our Lord never studied at the schools of the rabbis (John 7:15), but He taught with complete authority (Matt. 7:28–29). Even the greatest human teachers have to correct their work. In the year 426 the learned Augustine published his *Retractions* where he pointed out errors in his earlier books. But our Lord never needed to do this, for He was conscious of no error in His teaching. His teaching is perfect, eternally so (Matt. 24:35).

The whole Bible proclaims that Christ is indeed God. The kingdom of God is also the kingdom of the Son of Man (Matt. 13:41; 16:28; 25:31–46). The judgment seat of God (Rom. 14:10) is also the judgment seat of Christ (2 Cor. 5:10), for God and Christ share the one throne (Rev. 22:3). In the original Greek, when Paul wrote of God the Father and the Lord Jesus, he sometimes used a singular verb (1 Thess. 3:11; 2 Thess. 2:16–17). He did this because he thought of them as one in essence.

As we have already seen, there are indications in the Old Testament that the coming Messiah was divine. The angel of Jehovah is also Jehovah (e.g. Gen. 16:7,13; 32:24,30). The Messiah is called God in Psalm 45:6 and Isaiah 9:6, and His Kingdom is said to be eternal in Daniel 2:44; 7:13–14 and Micah 5:2. In Zechariah 12 God speaks (v. 1) and says that the inhabitants of Jerusalem 'will look on Me whom they have pierced' (v. 10), a prophecy which was fulfilled at the crucifixion of Christ (John 19:37). In Malachi 3:1 the prophet predicts that

God's messenger would come before God Himself came to His temple. This messenger would be like the prophet Elijah (Mal. 4:5–6). Thus when Jesus said that John the Baptist was this Elijah-like messenger, He was also identifying Himself as God (Matt. 11:14).

The deity of Christ can also be seen in the way that the New Testament uses the Old Testament. Isaiah 45:23 speaks of every knee bowing to God and every tongue confessing Him. In Romans 14:11 this is quoted as applying to God, but in Phil. 2:10–11 Paul applies it also to Christ. Boasting in Jehovah in the Old Testament (Jer. 9:24) is the same as boasting in Christ in the New (1 Cor. 1:31). God calls Himself 'the first and the last' in Isa. 44:6 and 48:12, and in the book of Revelation Christ speaks of Himself in the same terms (Rev. 1:17; 22:13; see also 1:8; 21:6).

In biblical times, people who were led to trust in Christ for salvation were also led to worship Him. This can be seen in Matthew 2:11; 8:2; 9:18; 14:33; 15:25; 20:20; 28:9,17; Luke 24:51–52; John 9:35–38 (see the A.V.). Even the angels worship Him (Heb. 1:6). Yet the Bible teaches that God is a jealous God (Ex. 20:5) who will not give His glory to another (Isa. 42:8). God, and God alone, is to be worshipped (Deut. 6:13; Matt. 4:10). When Cornelius tried to worship Peter, Peter stopped him, saying 'Stand up; I too am just a man.' (Acts 10:25–26). Paul and Barnabas also refused to accept worship from the heathen people of Lystra (Acts 14:11–15). Not even the angels are to be worshipped (Col. 2:18; Rev. 19:10; 22:8–9). But while the apostles and the angels refused to accept worship, Christ never refused it. Instead, the Lord Jesus taught that 'not even the Father judges any one, but He has given all judgment to the Son, in order that all may honour the Son, even as they honour the Father. He who does not honour the Son does not honour the Father who sent Him' (John 5:22–23).

Some of the people who demanded that Jesus should be crucified understood Him better than some who are supposed to be serving Him in the Church. Jesus' enemies knew that He was claiming to be God, but they thought that this was blasphemy (Matt. 26:63–66; John 5:18; 8:58–59; 10:33; 19:7). The One who claims to be God must either be the Christ (Matt. 16:16; Mark 14:61–64) or the Antichrist (2 Thess. 2:3–4). He must be worshipped as Lord and God (John 20:28) or stoned as a blasphemer (Lev. 24.16). But the Christian knows no such dilemma. He confesses Christ as 'God of God, Light of Light, Very God of Very God'. And he lifts up his voice in worship,

> 'Christ, our God, to Thee we raise
> This our sacrifice we praise.'

3. *'Behold, the Man!'*
The Bible teaches that during the reign of

Augustus Caesar (27 BC–14 AD), God the Son became a man (Luke 2:1; John 1:14). While He was in heaven, Christ existed in the form of God (Phil. 2:6), but when He became a man, He became a true man. He who is God is now also man, and will return in the form of a man (Matt. 24:30; Acts 1:11). The Lord Jesus referred to Himself as a man (John 8:40), and both His followers and His enemies did likewise (John 9:29; 19:5; Acts 2:22; Rom. 5:15; 1 Tim. 2:5). We have no physical description of Jesus, although there are hints that there was nothing particularly attractive about his appearance (Isa. 53:2–3). He may have looked much older than He was, humanly speaking (Luke 3:23; John 8:56–57).

As God, Christ is equal with the Father (John 10:30), but as man He is under the Father (John 14:28; 1 Cor. 11:3). In fact, while He was on earth, our Lord was made lower than the angels (Heb. 2:9), so much so that in the Garden of Gethsemane an angel came to comfort and strengthen Him (Luke 22:43).

To save man, God had to become man (Heb. 2:14–17). As a man, Christ was born (Matt. 2:1), He grew up (Luke 2:40,52), He became weary (John 4:6), He slept (Matt. 8:24), He was sometimes hungry or thirsty (Matt. 4:2; 21:18; John 4:7; 19:28), and at Lazarus' tomb He wept (John 11:35). At times the Bible gives us a very earthy picture of the Lord Jesus. The eternal Son of God spat on the ground before He performed some healings (Mark 7:33; John 9:6). He could be heard, seen and handled (Luke 24:39; John 20:27; 1 John 1:1), like any other man. He was tempted (Matt. 4:1–11; Heb. 2:18; 4:15), and He did not know the date of His coming again (Mark 13:32).

We have arrived at the edge of the deepest mystery – as a man, Christ was born of Mary (Luke 2:7), as God, He had no father or mother (Heb. 7:3); as man, He grew up (Luke 2:52), as God, He does not change (Heb. 13:8); as man, He slept in a boat (Matt. 8:24), as God, He upholds the universe by His power (Col. 1:17; Heb. 1:3); as man, He died (Luke 23:46), as God, He lives for ever (Heb. 7:3,22–25).

There have been people who have believed that Christ is both God and man, but they have combined the two natures into one. When this is done, the humanity is lost in the divinity, like rain falling on an ocean. We must be careful to worship Christ in two natures, as true God and true man.

> 'Lo! within a manger lies
> He who built the starry skies'.

We shall see later that the marvel of His person will lead us to the marvel of His work – to Jesus forsaken of God in order that His people might be saved (Matt. 27:46).

[45]

4. *The Titles of Jesus*

To help us understand something of Jesus, many titles are used of Him in Scripture. Some of the more important of these are:

(a) *Christ or Messiah.* The Greek word 'Christ' and the Hebrew word 'Messiah' both mean 'the anointed one'. Jesus used this title to describe Himself (Matt. 16:16–17; Mark 14:61–62; John 4:25–26). In the Old Testament, prophets (1 Kings 19:16), priests (Ex. 28:41; 29:7; Lev. 4:3) and kings (1 Sam. 9:16; 10:1; 16:12–13; 24:6) were anointed with oil. Jesus was anointed with the Holy Spirit to be prophet (one who teaches God's Word), priest (one who offers sacrifice to God), and king (the one who rules in the kingdom of God). At one time Jesus did not want His disciples to tell others that He was the Messiah (e.g. Mark 8:29–30). This was probably because many Jews wanted an earthly king who could drive the Romans from Palestine (John 6:15), not a king whose kingdom is not of this world (John 18:36). On one occasion, Jesus even kept His deity from a man who did not realize his need for Him (Mark 10:17–27).[1]

(b) *Son of God.* The term 'Son of God' or a similar title is applied to the people of Israel (Ex. 4:22; Hos. 11:1), the king (2 Sam. 7:14), angels (Job 1:6;

[1] The meaning of Mark 10:18 is not 'I am God, so you should not call me "good"', but 'You should not call me good unless you know that I am God.'

2:1), Adam (Luke 3:38), judges (Ps. 82:6), and Christian believers (Rom. 8:15–17; Gal. 4:5–7). In fact, in one sense all men are the offspring of God (Acts 17:28). But Jesus is the Son of God in a very different sense. The Son fully knows the Father (Matt. 11:27), for He is equal with the Father (John 5:18).

(c) *Son of Man.* This was Jesus' usual title for Himself. It is found eighty-nine times in the book of Ezekiel where it simply means 'man' or even 'mortal man' (e.g. Ezek. 2:1,3,6). But in Daniel 7:13–14 it is used to describe the One whose kingdom will last for ever (see Matt. 26:64). So this title points both to Jesus' humanity (e.g. Matt. 8:20) and His divinity (e.g. John 3:13).

(d) *Lord.* Sometimes this word (in Greek it is *kyrios*) only means 'Sir', and is used of men like Philip (John 12:21) and Paul and Silas (Acts 16:30). Even when it is used of Jesus, it sometimes still only means 'Sir' (e.g. John 4:11,15). But it is also a name for God, and it is used of Jesus in this sense in John 9:38; 20:28; and Philippians 2:9–11. In the middle of the second century a Christian leader named Polycarp of Smyrna was burnt at the stake for refusing to say 'Caesar is Lord'. Polycarp knew that Jesus will not share His Lordship with another (1 Cor. 8:6).

(e) *God.* As we have already seen, Jesus is often called God in the Scriptures (John 1:1,18; 20:28;

Rom. 9:5; Phil. 2:6; Tit. 2:13; Heb. 1:8; 2 Pet. 1:1). He is also called 'Immanuel' which means 'God with us' (Matt. 1:23).

5. *Stone of Stumbling or Chief Cornerstone?*

Christ Jesus is God and man, two natures united in the one Person. He is thus David's Lord and David's son (Matt. 22:41–46). This is the most extraordinary claim ever made in history, and it demands our response. To those who reject Him, Christ is a stone of stumbling, but to those who believe, He is the chief cornerstone (1 Pet. 2:7–8). While He was here on earth, some of His friends, perhaps even His family, thought that He was out of His mind (Mark 3:21, see John 7:5). Many others thought that He was of the devil (Matt. 12:24; John 8:52). But those who know and love Him will sing with Charles Wesley,

> 'Veiled in flesh the Godhead see;
> Hail, the Incarnate Deity,
> Pleased as Man with man to dwell,
> Jesus, our Immanuel!'

FOR FURTHER READING:
The Divine Glory of Christ, Charles J. Brown (Banner of Truth 1982)
The Lord from Heaven, Leon Morris (IVP 1958)

4

THE ATONEMENT

1. *Sinners in the Hands of an Angry God*

Martin Luther once commented that 'the cross of Christ runs through the whole of Scripture'. Whenever the apostles summarized the gospel, they always spoke of Christ's death and resurrection (e.g. Acts 2:22–24; 1 Cor. 15:3–4). Paul could even tell the Corinthians, 'I determined to know nothing among you except Jesus Christ, and Him crucified' (1 Cor. 2:2). This great emphasis on the cross goes back to Christ Himself. As the Lord Jesus thought of His own death, He wondered momentarily whether He might be spared the horror of the cross. But He knew that that could not be, for His whole purpose in coming to earth was to die thus (John 12:27). The Son of Man came specifically to give His life as a ransom for many (Mark 10:45; see Mark 8:31; 9:31; 10:33–34). Hence, any suggestion that He might avoid the cross could only come from Satan (Matt. 16:21–23).

The cross of Christ is central to the Christian faith. It is the cross that shall bring either condemnation or salvation to each one of us (1 Cor. 1:18). God the Son left the glory of heaven to endure being condemned as a criminal, being mocked and spat upon, having iron spikes driven through His hands and feet, suffering thirst and fever, and, worst of all, being forsaken by God the Father (see Ps. 22; Matt. 27:27–31,46). The thought of this moved Charles Wesley to write:

> "Tis mystery all! The Immortal dies:
> Who can explore His strange design?
> In vain the first-born seraph tries
> To sound the depths of love divine.'

But before we try to explore 'His strange design', we need to understand something of the holiness of God and the sinfulness of sin.

God is altogether holy. Both Testaments apply the anthem 'Holy, Holy, Holy' to Him (Isa. 6:3; Rev. 4:8). Because God's nature is holy, it follows that His law is holy and righteous and good — perfect, in fact (Rom. 7:12; Ps. 19:7). In keeping this law, there is life (Lev. 18:5; Ezek. 20:11; Rom. 2:13; 10:5). We should be clear about this, however. God is perfect and so demands that we be perfect (Matt. 5:48). It is not enough that we think we do more good deeds than bad; we must be perfect. God's perfect holiness necessarily means that He has a holy hatred of sin (Ps. 5:5; 7:11; note Ps. 97:10). Therefore, sin must meet with judgment, for God cannot bear the presence of evil-doers (Ex. 34:7; Isa. 59:2; Ezek. 24:13; Nah. 1:2; Hab. 1:13; Rom. 1:18; Heb. 2:2–3). It is not possible for anything unclean ever to enter the New Jerusalem (Rev. 21:27).

'There is a city bright;
Closed are its gates to sin;
Nought that defileth,
Nought that defileth
Can ever enter in.'

Many people think that because God is good, He
must forgive sin, but that is the wrong starting-
point. As John Murray put it, 'The question is not
at all: How can God, being what He is, send men
to hell? The question is: How can God, being what
He is, save them from hell?' There are some things
God cannot do — He cannot look on wickedness
(Hab. 1:13), He cannot deny Himself (2 Tim. 2:13),
and He cannot lie (Heb. 6:18; Tit. 1:2). In short,
God cannot live with sin for that would be to deny
His own holy nature.

When God created the first man Adam, He created
him good (Gen. 1:26; Eccles. 7:29). The Lord then
commanded him, saying, 'From any tree of the garden
you may eat freely; but from the tree of the knowledge
of good and evil you shall not eat, for in the day that
you eat from it you shall surely die' (Gen. 2:16–17).
God commanded Adam to obey him, and he had the
power to do so. But he fell into sin— he disobeyed God
and ate the forbidden fruit (Gen. 3:5–6). Sin had
invaded the earth! From this time on, man was subject
to death as the penalty for sin. This death includes
physical death (the separation of the soul from the
body), spiritual death (the separation of the soul from

God), and eternal death (the eternal separation of body and soul from God).

Adam's guilt and corruption spread to all men (Rom. 5:12–19; 1 Cor. 15:22).

> 'In Adam's fall,
> We sinned all.'

We are all conceived and born in sin (Ps. 51:5) and so by nature are under God's wrath (Eph. 2:3). Of ourselves, we do not please God; in fact, we cannot please Him (Rom. 8:8). Even our good intentions can lead us astray (Prov. 14:12), and our best actions are full of evil (Isa. 64:6). The fact that we bring earthly good to others does not change our evil natures (Matt. 7:11). The fault lies not only in what we do but what we are deep down in our hearts (Jer. 17:9; Prov. 4:23; Mark 7:20–23). A radical defilement stains every man, woman and child who is descended from Adam (Gen. 8:21; 1 Kings 8:46; Ps. 130:3; Prov. 20:9; Mark 10:18; Rom. 3:9–12,23; Gal. 3:22). As Augustine pointed out, even the baby at the breast is bound in sin.

This leaves us in a dreadful situation, for if we fail to keep God's law perfectly we fall under God's curse (Deut. 27:26; Gal. 3:10). This curse is death (Gen. 2:16–17; Ezek. 18:4,20; Rom. 6:23)– physical death (e.g. Gen. 5:5), spiritual death (Eph. 2:1) and eternal death (Rev. 21:8). The law, which should have brought us life, now brings death (Rom. 7:9–13). Indeed, because of sin, it has become 'the ministry of death' (2 Cor. 3:7). We all face death and judgment at the hands of God who is a consuming fire (Heb. 9:27; 12:29). No wonder that Hebrews 10:31 tells us that 'It is a terrifying thing to fall into the hands of the living God.' Sinful man is totally unable to redeem himself (Ps. 49:7–9). Realizing this, Job cried out, 'How can a man be in the right before God?' (Job 9:2). In Anselm's language, man's problem is that he has a debt to God which he must pay, but which only God is able to pay (see Matt. 18:23–35). Job saw that we need a mediator, one who might lay his hand upon both God and man, and bring the two together (Job 9:32–33).

This mediator must be perfect, not subject to sin's curse. This means He must be God. Yet He must also be able to pay the penalty for sin which is death. Since God cannot die, the mediator must be a man. He must be the God-Man. We have already seen that Jesus Christ is such a Mediator (1 Tim. 2:5). His work of salvation is a work of substitution – 'Christ died for the ungodly' (Rom. 5:6), 'the just for the unjust' (1 Pet. 3:18). Christ thus came to do what the law could not do because of our sin (Acts 13:39; Rom. 8:3–4) – He came to make an atonement for sin and bring sinners back to God.

2. *The Death of Christ*

By some Christ's death is only seen as the supreme example of loving self-sacrifice. It is true that our Lord left us an example to follow (1 Pet. 2:21; 1

John 3:16), but the main emphasis in Scripture is on His death as an atonement for sin (e.g. Isa. 53:4–6,10,12; 2 Cor. 5:21; 1 Pet. 2:24). This teaching has always offended some and been considered foolish by others (1 Cor. 1:23–24). Rudolf Bultmann, for example, has exclaimed, 'What a primitive mythology it is, that a divine Being should become incarnate, and atone for the sins of men through His own blood!' Even true Christians are often rather vague about the workings of the atonement. C. S. Lewis was content to say that the death of Christ brings salvation to believers in Him; he did not want to explore how this is achieved.

The Bible presents the truth of the atonement in many ways:

(a) *Obedience.* The basis for the atonement lies in Christ's obedience. 'For as through the one man's disobedience the many were made sinners, even so through the obedience of the One the many will be made righteous' (Rom. 5:19). Throughout His life Christ always did the will of His Father (John 4:34; 6:38). This obedience to the Father's will culminated in Christ's death on the cross (Matt. 26:39; Acts 2:23; Phil. 2:7–8; Heb. 5:8–9; 10:8–10). Christ's obedience unto death was totally voluntary (John 10:17–18).

Our Lord is the only man who has fulfilled Romans 2:13 ('doers of the law will be justified') and who is not subject to Ezekiel 18:4 ('the soul who sins will die'). Man's death comes because of his disobedience, but Christ's death was the result of His obedience.

> 'There was no other good enough
> To pay the price of sin;
> He only could unlock the gate
> Of heaven, and let us in.'

(b) *Sacrifice.* During the Old Testament period, many sacrifices were offered to God. In fact, these were offered morning and evening each day (Num. 28:4). The idea behind these sacrifices was that in the shedding of blood the penalty for sin (death) was paid (Lev. 17:11; see Lev. 4:20,26,31). This was clearly understood on the annual Day of Atonement when one goat was slain for the sins of the people, while another sin-bearing goat was released (Lev. 16). Actually the Old Testament sacrifices were never more than shadows or pictures of the true sacrifice (Col. 2:17; Heb. 9:23–24; 10:1). As Calvin said, 'There could be nothing more silly and frivolous than to offer the fat and stinking entrails of beasts in order to reconcile oneself with God'. Hebrews 10:4 tells us that 'it is impossible for the blood of bulls and goats to take away sins.'

The Old Testament sacrifices were designed by God to point to the sacrifice of Christ. Christ, our High Priest, is eternal (Heb. 7:3,24–25) and sinless (Heb. 7:26–27). Therefore, His sacrifice for sin is perfect, and offered once for all (Heb. 7:27; 10:10). His cross abolished the Old Testament sacrifices

(Heb. 10:18). True believers in the Old Testament period were in reality saved, not by the various sacrifices, but by Christ's sacrifice (Heb. 9:15).

Christ is thus the Lamb of God offered for the sins of His people (John 1:29,36). The slaying of the Passover lambs preserved the Israelites from death in Exodus 12, but this really pointed to Christ, the true Passover Lamb (1 Cor. 5:7). His blood obtained eternal redemption for his people. (1 Pet. 1:18–19; Heb. 9:12).

(c) *Propitiation.* This is the key to understanding the death of Christ. We have seen that God is filled with a holy wrath against sin. This wrath must be appeased or propitiated if man is to be saved. The Bible teaches that on the cross Christ was set forth as a *propitiation* (Rom. 3:25; see also 1 John 2:2; 4:10). Many modern translations avoid this word because the translators do not like to think that God is angry with sin.[1] But on the cross Christ was forsaken by God (Matt. 27:46) and under His curse (Gal. 3:13). God treated Christ as a sinner – indeed, as sin itself – although Christ had never sinned (2 Cor. 5:21). In a sense, Christ was treated like the

[1] In Rom. 3:25 the A.V. and the N.A.S.B. have 'propitiation'. The R.S.V. has 'expiation', the G.N.B. has 'the means by which people's sins are forgiven', and the N.I.V. has 'a sacrifice of atonement'. *The Living Bible* has, correctly, references to God's anger, but adds, 'He (God) used Christ's blood and our faith as the means of saving us from His wrath.' This confuses the basis (Christ's death) and the means (our faith).

serpent, (John 3:14–15; Num. 21:4–9). The thought of all this moved James Henley Thornwell to ask, 'Who, at the foot of Calvary, can pronounce sin to be a light matter?' Golgotha shows us just how much God hates sin.

Propitiation has been both misunderstood and misrepresented. In enduring all the righteous fury of God against sin, Christ did not win the love of God but satisfied the justice of God. It is the sinner that is forgiven, not the sin. The sin had to be punished. But at Calvary God propitiated Himself. The Son did not make the Father loving; it was because the Father was loving that He sent the Son to be the propitiation for His people's sins (1 John 4:10). God's holiness requires that He punish sin, but out of His mercy He provided an atonement for sin. Both His holy justice and His loving kindness are revealed at Calvary.

> 'What glad return can I impart
> For favours so divine?
> O take my all, this worthless heart,
> And make it only Thine.'
>
> (Anne Steele)

(d) *Reconciliation.* Sin separates God and man (Isa. 59:2), and so makes them enemies (Rom. 5:10). But in the death of Christ the people of God are reconciled to Him and He is reconciled to them (Rom. 5:8–11; 2 Cor. 5:18–20). It is the blood of the cross that brings peace between God and man

(Col. 1:20–22). We should not think that Christ's death only causes the change in the believer's attitude to God. That is true, but it also reconciles God to man. It is difficult to understand, but before God calls a person to faith in Christ, He both loves that person and is angry with that person (Rom. 5:8–10; Eph. 2:3). A parent knows something of this when he is angry with a sinning child.

(e) *Redemption.* All who sin are slaves to sin (John 8:34), but Christ paid the ransom price which brings freedom to the Christian (Mark 10:45; Acts 20:28; 1 Tim. 2:6; Tit. 2:14). That is why Christians are said to be bought with a price (1 Cor. 6:19–20), the price of Jesus' own blood (Eph. 1:7; 1 Pet. 1:18–19; Rev. 5:9). Many of the Fathers of the early Church thought that the ransom was paid to the devil, but instead, it should be thought of as being paid to God. The devil has no rights over God's creation. However, redemption does mean freedom from the power of Satan. On the cross Christ triumphed over Satan (John 12:31; Col. 2:15). Man's slavery to sin and death was ended.

To summarize, Christ's death was an act of substitution in which our Lord bore the guilt of His people, endured the wrath of God, overcame the hostility between God and man, and ended man's bondage to Satan.

'Guilty, vile, and helpless we;
Spotless Lamb of God was He:

Full atonement – can it be?
Hallelujah! what a Saviour!'
(Philip P. Bliss)

3. Is the Atonement Perfect?

The question as to the perfection of the atonement amounts to this: 'Did Christ obtain salvation for His people or did He only obtain the possibility of salvation?' Many teach that man must add something to the finished work of Christ, whether this be works or faith. You might have heard hymns like this:

'Christ is knocking at my sad heart;
Shall I let Him in?
Patiently knocking at my sad heart,
Oh, shall I let Him in?'

Such hymns leave us with the impression that Christ has done all He could to save us; the rest is up to us. It is as if Christ put the key into the door of heaven, and then left us to decide whether we would turn it or not.

But the whole Bible teaches that our Lord actually saves, not that He offers the possibility of salvation (Matt. 1:21; Gal. 2:21; 5:2,4; Eph. 1:7; Col. 2:13-14). If we are Christ's, then no sin can possibly be laid to our charge (Rom. 8:33–34). The penalty for sin has been paid in full.

'If Thou hast my discharge procured,
And freely in my room endured
The whole of wrath divine;

[59]

Payment God cannot twice demand –
First at my bleeding Surety's hand,
And then again at mine.'
(Augustus M. Toplady)

Christ's one offering has perfected for all time those who are being sanctified (Heb. 10:14). Because Christ is fully divine (Col. 2:9), He brings a full salvation (Col. 2:10). His blood cleanses from all sin – past, present and future (1 John 1:7). The sacrifice of the Lord Jesus has infinite value, so we cannot add anything to it.

'Thou, O Christ, art all I want;
More than all in Thee I find'
(Charles Wesley)

There is, however, a verse – Colossians 1:24 – that needs to be explained. Here Paul says, 'I fill up in my flesh what is still lacking in regard to Christ's afflictions, for the sake of his body, which is the church' (NIV). This passage is not speaking of the atonement but of the work of evangelism. The afflictions that Christ suffers here are the afflictions that His body, the Church, suffers. When Saul was busy ravaging the Church (Acts 8:3), he was also persecuting the Lord Jesus Himself, the King and Head of the Church (Acts 9:5).

The true gospel is that Jesus saves, not that He helps bring about salvation. The Puritan writer John Owen well understood this. He wrote, 'Christ hath obtained salvation for men, not upon condition if they would receive it, but so fully and perfectly that certainly they should receive it.'

4. *For whom did Christ Die?*

Our answer to this question will be closely related to our answer to the question raised in section 3. There are three logical possibilities:

(1) If Christ's atonement is perfect, and He died for all men, then all men must be saved.

(2) If Christ died for all men, but not all are saved, then His atonement cannot be perfect.

(3) If Christ's atonement is perfect, and not all men are saved, then His atonement can only have been intended for His chosen ones, the elect.

The Bible, in fact, teaches this third position — Christ only died for those who will be saved. These are His people (Isa. 53:8; Matt. 1:21), His sheep (John 10:11,15), the Church (Acts 20:28; Eph. 5:25), those who die to self in Him (2 Cor. 5:14–15). He died for those for whom He prayed — not for the world, but for those whom the Father had given to Him (John 17:9).

Christ redeems those whom the Father predestined to salvation before the foundation of the world (Eph. 1:4–5). The Father chose His people before they had done anything good or bad (Rom. 9:10–13); it was all of his sheer unmerited grace, nothing of works (Rom. 11:6). Such a choice was well-pleasing in the Father's sight (Matt. 11:25–26).

As a result, the Christian does not *let* Christ into

his heart; rather, it is the case that we cannot come to Him unless it has been granted to us from the Father (John 6:65; Acts 13:48). Today, many teach that 'If you believe, then Christ died for you.' But the Bible teaches, 'If Christ died for you, then you will believe.' There are unbreakable links in the chain of salvation, from God's foreknowledge and predestination to the Christian's glorification in heaven (Rom. 8:29–30). All whom God has fore-known are predestined, called, justified, and finally glorified. Although glorification refers to a future event, Paul spoke of it as if it had already happened, so certain was he that it would happen (Rom. 8:30). The good Shepherd cannot lose one of His predes-tined sheep (John 10:27–29; 18:9).

There are some Bible passages that are used to support the view that Christ died for everybody:

(a) John 3:16 says that 'God so loved the world', but here 'the world' does not mean everybody in it, any more than John 1:10 means that everybody in the world rejected Christ. It probably only means that Gentiles as well as Jews were included in God's love.

(b) 1 Timothy 2:4 says that God 'desires all men to be saved and to come to the knowledge of the truth'. This passage is concerned with prayer and the offer of salvation, not with the extent of the atonement. The meaning is that all kinds of men may be saved, even ungodly kings. A Christian should pray for them for God may be gracious to them (1 Tim. 2:1–4). Similarly, in Acts 2:17 where God pours out His Spirit upon 'all flesh', the meaning is that all kinds of people received the Spirit.

(c) 1 John 2:1–2 is another passage which has been misunderstood. John here directs sinning Christians to the work of Christ. It would be a strange comfort indeed if John's meaning is that Christ is the propitiation for the sins of all men, even the damned. What John obviously means is that Christ is the only propitiation for the sins of all who believe in Him, no matter where they be in the world.

(d) Finally, there is 2 Peter 2:1 which refers to heretics denying the Master who bought them. This only refers to the heretics in the way in which they would have referred to themselves when they first professed themselves disciples of Christ.

When we consider the doctrine of God's predestination, we must not begin by asking, 'Did God choose me before I was born?' Rather, we must first look to the Lord Jesus Christ, His death for sinners, and His promise that 'the one who comes to Me I will certainly not cast out' (John 6:37). We must believe before we can know of our election. As John Newton put it,

> 'Approach, my soul, the mercy-seat,
>   Where Jesus answers prayer;
>   There humbly fall before His feet,
>   For none can perish there.

Thy promise is my only plea;
With this I venture nigh:
Thou callest burdened souls to Thee,
And such, O Lord, am I.'

Many people, even some Christians, reject the doctrine that Christ died only for the elect. This was so in the apostle Paul's day too (see Rom. 9:14,19). But Paul's answer is God's answer, and it must silence all our objections: 'Who are you, O man, who answers back to God?' (Rom. 9:20). We ought to imitate Augustine who wrote of this doctrine, 'O depth! Do you seek a reason? I will tremble at the depth. Do you reason? I will wonder. Do you dispute? I will believe.' Then we will understand why Luther called predestination 'the sweetest of all doctrines', for it teaches that our salvation is totally in God's hands and His love is from everlasting (Jer. 31:3).

5. *Who Pays?*

Many centuries ago Anselm of Canterbury wrote a treatise on the atonement, and warned that 'we must recognize that, whatever a man can say on this subject, the deeper reasons for so great a thing remain hidden.' It is indeed a mystery! God did not need to save anyone, for He is complete in Himself; He has no need of anything (Acts 17:25). Yet, out of His grace, He planned to save a people for Himself. To do this, it was necessary that God the Son should die. Christ prayed that, if possible, another way might be found, but this was not possible (Matt. 26:39). No law exists which could give life to sinful man (Gal. 3:21). So the Son of Man had to die.

Man's guilt had to be expiated and God's wrath propitiated. In short, God had to be both just and the justifier (Rom. 3:26). He had to be just in punishing sin, and the justifier in forgiving sinners who have faith in Jesus. At the cross of Christ, God's holy righteousness and His abounding mercy were both clearly demonstrated.

Sin must still be paid for. Either we pay for it, eternally, or we accept Christ's gracious payment for it. All the sins of God's people are laid upon Christ, and all His righteousness is laid upon those who trust in Him. This is Christ's work of substitution. The curse which lies upon sinners (Gal. 3:10) was taken upon Himself by Christ (Gal. 3:13).

> 'Thy grief and bitter passion
> Were all for sinners' gain;
> Mine, mine was the transgression,
> But Thine the deadly pain.'
> (Paul Gerhardt)

FOR FURTHER READING:
Redemption: Accomplished and Applied, John Murray
   (Banner of Truth 1979)
The Atonement, Leon Morris (IVP 1984)

5

THE PERSON AND WORK OF
THE HOLY SPIRIT

1. *The Person of the Holy Spirit*

Section 6 of 'the Triune God' has shown us that the Holy Spirit is God. This section will add more of the Biblical evidence:

(a) The third Person of the Trinity is the Spirit of the Lord, but He is also the Lord (2 Cor. 3:17–18), just as the Word of God is God (John 1:1).

(b) Since the three Persons of the Holy Trinity are equal, the Christian, who has the Spirit in him (John 14:16–17), also has the Father and the Son in him (John 14:23).[1]

(c) The Spirit is called 'another Helper' (or Comforter or Intercessor) in John 14:16, which shows that He is what Christ is. This means that He is divine. Therefore, having the Spirit in us is the same as having Christ in us (Rom. 8:9–11), and hearing what Christ says to the churches (Rev. 1:1,11–20; chapters 2–3) is the same as hearing what the Spirit says to the churches (Rev. 2:7,11,17,29; 3:6,13,22). Like Christ (John 1:18), the Spirit reveals God to His people (1 Cor. 2:10–14).

---

[1] Hence the Spirit of God is sometimes called the Spirit of Christ or the Spirit of the Son (Acts 16:7; Rom. 8:9; Gal. 4:6; Phil. 1:19).

(d) A Christian's body is the temple of God (1 Cor. 3:16–17)[2] or the temple of the Holy Spirit (1 Cor. 6:19).

(e) All Scripture is inspired by God (2 Tim. 3:16), and so can be attributed to the Holy Spirit (e.g. Matt. 22:43; Acts 1:16; 4:25; Heb. 3:7; 10:15–17). Similarly, prophecy can be said to have come from God (Jer. 1:5,9; 23:21), Christ (Matt. 23:34; Eph. 4:11) and the Holy Spirit (1 Pet. 1:10–11; 2 Pet. 1:21).

The Holy Spirit might be called the hidden Person of the Holy Trinity. He brings glory to Christ, not to Himself (John 15:26; 16:14). Yet He is truly God and His work is truly divine. The Scriptures teach us that God the Father planned the redemption of His people, God the Son achieved it, and God the Holy Spirit applies it. One of Charles Wesley's hymns, speaking of the work of the Spirit in the life of a Christian, tells us this:

'God, through Himself, we then shall know,
If Thou within us shine,
And sound, with all Thy saints below,
The depths of love divine.'

2. *The Holy Spirit Before Pentecost*

We should not think that the Holy Spirit came down to earth for the first time on the Day of Pentecost (see Acts 2). We find that the Spirit was

[2] This is plural and refers to the Church, but the point is still valid.

present in the Old Testament period, in creation (Gen. 1:2; Job 33:4), in providing leaders for God's people (Judges 3:10; 6:34; 11:29; 13:25), giving strength and skill (Judges 14:19; Ex. 31:3–5), and in reviving the people of God (Ezek. 37:1–14). He was with all the Old Testament saints, notably Joseph (Gen. 41:38), Moses (Num. 11:16–17), Joshua (Deut. 34:9) and David (1 Sam. 16:13; hence David's prayer in Ps. 51:11 when he fell into great sin). Furthermore, it was the Spirit who inspired the prophets (Neh. 9:30; Ezek. 11:5; Mic. 3:7–8).

Yet during the Old Testament period it is clear that the Spirit had not come in all His fulness. The Old Testament prophets looked forward to a time when the Spirit would make Himself known in a greater way (Ezek. 36:26–27; Joel 2:28–29). This would happen when the Messiah came (Isa. 11:1), for He would have the Spirit (Isa. 11:2). Indeed, the Spirit was given to the Lord Jesus 'without measure' (John 3:34; see Luke 1:35; 3:21–22; 4:18; Matt. 12:28).

During the earthly ministry of Christ, the Spirit did not come to believers in all His fulness (John 7:37–39). It was thus to the advantage of Christians that Christ should return to His Father, so that the Spirit would come (John 16:7). After Christ was glorified, the Spirit came as promised, and will abide with Christians for ever (Acts 2; John 14:16). If we are Christians, we are not left as orphans; we have 'another Helper' with us, indeed, in us (John

14:16—18). He takes Christ's place on earth. That is why Tertullian, one of the Fathers in the early Church, referred to the Holy Spirit as 'the vicar of Christ'.

3. *The Spirit in the Life of the Individual Christian*

Before we look at the Spirit's work in the life of a Christian, it should be made very clear that it is Christ who saves the sinner. Sometimes you might hear someone teach that it is not enough for the sinner to come to Christ; he needs to go on to the Holy Spirit. This teaching is altogether wrong. The Holy Spirit does not add to the work of Christ for in Christ there is already the fulness of salvation (Col. 2:10). The Spirit only applies the work of Christ — He takes Christ's work and makes it known to His people (John 16:14).

This work of the Spirit is most necessary, for if the Spirit is not in us, we cannot be Christians (John 3:3—6; Rom. 8:9; 1 Cor. 2:14). The Christian life is begun in the Spirit (Gal. 3:3) and will be brought to its final glory in Him (Rom. 8:11). As Octavius Winslow has said, 'Not a step can the believer advance without the Spirit . . . As he needed Him at the first, so he needs Him all his journey through.'

When we discuss the work of the Spirit in the life of a Christian, we divide the work up in order to try to understand it better. But when the Spirit of God works in the soul of a person, many of these divisions may not be clear to that person. The work of the Spirit is a unity. In Abraham Kuyper's words, 'the operations of grace are riveted together as the links of a chain.' It is possible to have truly repented of our sin and to have cast ourselves upon the Lord Jesus for salvation, and yet not to know all the theological terms. To quote Kuyper again: 'He who breathes deeply unconscious of his lungs is often the healthiest.' The Spirit has worked in your life if you can say with all your heart,

> 'My hope is built on nothing less
> Than Jesus' blood and righteousness;
> I dare not trust the sweetest frame,
> But wholly lean on Jesus' Name.'

The links in the great chain of salvation are:

(a) *Calling*. There are two types of calling. God calls all men to repent and come to Christ for the forgiveness of their sins (Matt. 22:14; Acts 17:30). This is a work of the Holy Spirit, but it can be resisted (Acts 7:51). However, God's effectual call of those whom He has foreknown and predestined cannot be resisted (Rom. 8:29–30). Those whom God has chosen must respond to His call and be justified and finally glorified (Rom. 8:29–30; 11:29; 2 Tim. 1:9).

(b) *Regeneration*. This refers to the change which the Holy Spirit brings about in the whole life and disposition of a man. It is a most remarkable change – it is life from death (John 5:24; Col. 2:13), a rebirth (John 3:3), the passing of the old and the making of the new (2 Cor. 5:17), a movement from darkness to light (1 Pet. 2:9) and from hostility to God to love and holiness (Col. 1:21–22). This is the Holy Spirit's work (Ezek. 11:19; 36:26–27; John 3:5,6,8; Tit. 3:5); it does not come *from* any decision made by man (John 1:12–13). At the moment when the Spirit gives new life we do not co-operate with the Spirit – in fact, until we are made new we oppose Him (Rom. 8:5–8) – nor can we fully understand this re-birth (John 3:8).

If it has happened to us, we can only pray that it would happen to others:

> 'O Spirit of the Lord, prepare
> All the round earth her God to meet;
> Breathe Thou abroad like morning air,
> Till hearts of stone begin to beat.'

(c) *Repentance and Faith.* True repentance is a gift from the triune God (Acts 5:31; 11:18; 2 Tim. 2:25). More specifically, it is the Holy Spirit who convicts the world of sin, righteousness and judgment (John 16:8–11). There is much shallow thinking about repentance today. Men like Saul and Judas were sorry for what they did, but they never desired to see their sins put to death (1 Sam. 24: 17–22; 26:21; Matt. 27:3–5). True repentance is a searching work of the Holy Spirit; it is not simply a worldly sorrow which comes when things go wrong (2 Cor. 7:10). It is a crucifixion of the flesh with its passions and desires (Gal. 5:24). That is why Joseph Hart cried out to the Spirit,

> 'Convince us of our sin,
> Then lead to Jesus' blood,
> And to our wondering view reveal
> The secret love of God.'

Repentance goes hand-in-hand with faith. Faith, too, is a gift of God (John 6:37,44,65; Eph. 2:8; Phil. 1:29). Again it is only the Holy Spirit who can lead us to trust in Jesus as Lord (1 Cor. 12:3). He is the Spirit of faith, i.e. the Spirit who gives faith (2 Cor. 4:13). Faith comes from hearing the Word of God (Rom. 10:17), but, as always, God's Word and His Spirit go together (Prov. 1:23). The Holy Spirit gives faith to all for whom Christ died.

As faith grows, assurance of salvation comes to many Christians, although some never receive it (see Mark 9:24). Assurance grows as a Christian understands the love of God revealed in the death of Christ (Rom. 8:32), and as he grows in obedience to God's commandments (1 John 2:3,5) and in the love of Christian brethren (1 John 3:14). Assurance is also a work of the Holy Spirit (Rom. 8:16; 1 John 3:24; 4:13).

(d) *Justification.* Justification is not said to be specifically a work of the Holy Spirit, but we need to look at it briefly in order to understand the application of Christ's work. In justification, God declares that the sinner is not condemned but is righteous before the Almighty on the ground of the finished work of Christ. God does not make the sinner righteous, but declares him righteous – the opposite of 'to justify' is not 'to make evil' but 'to condemn' (see Rom. 8:33–34).

In justification, the perfect righteousness of Christ is credited to the sinner who has faith in Jesus (Rom. 3:21–22,24; 10:4; 2 Cor. 5:21; Phil. 3:9). Thus all sins – past, present and future – are forgiven. We speak of 'justification by faith', but we should be clear that our faith does not save us. It is Christ who saves. As B. B. Warfield put it, 'The saving power of faith resides . . . not in itself, but in the Almighty Saviour on whom it rests.'

Salvation comes to the sinner when God gives him the gift of faith in Christ. This gift comes of God's free grace. Our works earn His condemnation, not His mercy, so justification cannot come by keeping God's law (Rom. 3:20,28; Gal. 2:16). If we know our own hearts, we will know why Luther wrote,

> 'To wash away the crimson stain,
>   Grace, grace alone availeth;
>   Our works, alas! are all in vain;
>   In much the best life faileth:
>   No man can glory in Thy sight,
>   All must alike confess Thy might,
>   And live alone by mercy.'

(e) *Adoption*. If God has declared us righteous because of Christ, then we are adopted into His family. We receive a new status. In Adam, we are only children of His wrath (Eph. 2:3), but in Christ this is all changed. God the Father predestines the elect to adoption as sons through Jesus Christ (Eph. 1:5). The Spirit is sent that those who are in Christ might know that they are sons of the Father (Rom. 8:15–16; Gal. 4:5–6).

(f) *Sanctification*. By faith Augustus Toplady came to the cross of Christ with the prayer:

> 'Let the water and the blood,
> From Thy riven side which flowed,
> Be of sin the double cure,
> Cleanse me from its guilt and power.'

Essentially, justification refers to the sinner's guilt being forgiven, and sanctification to the breaking of the power of sin in the life of the Christian. Justification is an act, sanctification a process; justification is *for* us, sanctification is *in* us; justification is perfect, sanctification is incomplete in this life. Justification is like the wedding, sanctification is like the marriage.

In sanctification, a Christian puts off his old life (Col. 3:5–11) and puts on a new life (Col. 3:12–17). As Abraham Kuyper so beautifully put it, sanctification is 'the reflection of Christ's form upon the mirror-surface of the soul'. The Christian becomes conformed to the image of Christ (Rom. 8:29).

All our sanctification is in Christ (John 15:4; Acts 26:18; Rom. 6:6; 1 Cor. 1:30; Eph. 5:25–27; Tit. 2:14; Heb. 10:10), but it can be ascribed to God (1 Thess. 5:23), to Christ (1 Cor. 1:2) and more especially, to the Holy Spirit (Rom. 8:2–4; 14:17; 2 Cor. 3:18; Gal. 5:16–25; 2 Thess. 2:13; 1 Pet. 1:2). Again, the Spirit uses God's Word to sanctify the believer (John 17:17; 1 Pet. 1:22). Sanctification is not man's attempt to improve himself, but man is active, nevertheless (Rom. 8:13; 12:1–2,9,16–17; Eph. 6:10–18; Phil. 2:12–13; James 4:7).

A faith which comes from the Holy Spirit is not a dead faith (James 2:14,17,26), but works through love (Gal. 5:6). Salvation does not end at justification, for God has already prepared good works that the Christian should walk in them (Eph. 2:10).

A Christian who is uninterested in holiness is no true Christian. Sin grieves the Holy Spirit (Eph. 4:30), and must grieve the Christian too (Rom. 7:18–19). We need to remember that without sanctification no one will see the Lord (Heb. 12:14). A Christian will delight in the law of God (Rom. 7:22) and he will press on towards the goal which is Christ Jesus (Phil. 3:12–14). Hence Philip Doddridge's prayer:

> 'O may Thy Spirit seal our souls,
> And mould them to Thy will,
> That our weak hearts no more may stray,
> But keep Thy precepts still;

THE MILK OF THE WORD

> That to perfection's sacred height
> We nearer still may rise,
> And all we think, and all we do,
> Be pleasing in Thine eyes.'

(g) *Perseverance*. We have seen that those whom God has chosen from the foundation of the world must persevere to the end and be received into glory. It is not possible for the elect to fall away (Matt. 24:24) or be condemned (Rom. 8:33–34). Those professing Christians who fall away may have tasted of the heavenly gift (Heb. 6:4–6), but they were never truly in Christ (1 John 2:19). A true Christian is sealed with the Holy Spirit for the day of redemption (Eph. 1:13–14; 4:30). The Holy Spirit does not visit Christians but abides for ever (John 14:16–17). God's pledge cannot be broken (Eph. 1:14).

(h) *Glorification*. At glorification the believer's body is resurrected and he enters into the joy of the Lord. Just as Christ was resurrected by the Father (Acts 2:24; Eph. 1:20), by Christ Himself (John 10:17–18) and by the Holy Spirit (Rom. 8:11; 1 Pet. 3:18), so the believer's resurrection must be understood as a work of all three Persons of the Trinity.

4. *Other Aspects of the Spirit's Work*

There are many aspects of the Spirit's work which were not considered in the last section, especially with respect to His work in the Church.

[76]

> 'Come as the dove: and spread Thy wings,
> The wings of peaceful love;
> And let Thy Church on earth become
> Blest as the Church above.'

This work might be summarized as follows:

(a) The Spirit provides guidance for God's people (Acts 8:29; 10:19–20; 11:12; 16:6–7). Since we have the complete Scriptures now, He does not guide in exactly the same way, but He still leads His people today.

(b) The Spirit moves us to pray and then helps us in our prayers (Zech. 12:10; Rom. 8:26–27; Eph. 2:18; 6:18; Jude 20). As one hymn puts it,

> 'Holy Spirit, prompt us
> When we kneel to pray;
> Nearer come, and teach us
> What we ought to say.'

A Christian prays on the basis of the finished work of Christ (Heb. 10:19–22), and as the Holy Spirit helps him on earth, so Christ Himself intercedes for him in heaven (Heb. 7:25).

(c) The Spirit animates all true worship of God which is according to His Word (John 4:24; Phil. 3:3).

(d) Wherever fellowship in Christ is experienced, it is because the Spirit is present (2 Cor. 13:14; Phil. 2:1). Then the love of God is poured out within the hearts of Christians through the Holy Spirit (Rom. 5:5).

(e) It is the Spirit who preserves the unity of the one body of true believers in Christ (Eph. 4:4).

(f) Gifts are given to the Church in order that Christians might encourage and edify one another (1 Cor. 12:7; Eph. 4:11–12; 1 Pet. 4:10). These gifts come from God (Rom. 12:3–8; 1 Pet. 4:10), Christ (Eph. 4:8,11) and the Holy Spirit (1 Cor. 12:11). The greatest gift is prophecy (1 Cor. 14:1),[3] but the highest way is love (1 Cor. 13). No Christian has every gift (1 Cor. 12:29–30) but all Christians should exhibit the moral fruit of the Spirit in their lives (Gal. 5:22–23).

> 'I ask no dream, no prophet-ecstasies,
> No sudden rending of the veil of clay,
> No angel-visitant, no opening skies;
> But take the dimness of my soul away.'

Many people today emphasize the more spectacular gifts like healing and speaking in tongues. But the ability to perform signs and wonders was given to apostles rather than to all Christians (Rom. 15:18–19; 2 Cor. 12:12). An unconverted man may still be able to speak in tongues, even the tongues of angels (1 Cor. 13:1). He may even be able to heal in Jesus' name (Matt. 7:22–23). Even in apostolic days, the ability to speak in tongues was the least of the gifts (1 Cor. 12:28–30); it is not even mentioned in Romans 12:6–8 and Ephesians 4:11. Paul points

[3] Whatever else prophecy refers to, it clearly points to rational and intelligible preaching of God's Word.

out that speaking in tongues does not edify others (1 Cor. 14:1–5), it is unintelligible unless it is properly interpreted (1 Cor. 14:6–19), it is useless for evangelism (1 Cor. 14:23–25), and it can be disruptive of church order (1 Cor. 14:26–40). Let us seek the greater gifts – to speak the truth in love and so grow up in all aspects into Him who is the head, even Christ (Eph. 4:15).

5. *From Him and through Him and to Him*

When the apostle Peter wrote to the Christians of Pontus, Galatia, Cappadocia, Asia and Bithynia, he referred to them as 'chosen according to the foreknowledge of God the Father, by the sanctifying work of the Spirit, that you may obey Jesus Christ and be sprinkled with His blood' (1 Pet. 1:1–2). Peter was making it very obvious to his readers that, from beginning to end, salvation is a work of the Triune God, that from Him and through Him and to Him are all things (Rom. 11:36). The Christian is, in Augustine's words, 'predestined by grace, and chosen by grace, by grace a pilgrim below, and by grace a citizen above.'

If the Holy Spirit does indwell us, then we will join with Joseph Hart in the prayer:

> 'Dwell, therefore, in our hearts;
> Our minds from bondage free;
> Then shall we know and praise and love
> The Father, Son, and Thee.'

FOR FURTHER READING:

The Work of the Holy Spirit, Octavius Winslow (Banner of Truth 1984)

Signs of the Apostles, Walter J. Chantry (Banner of Truth 1976)

Spirit of the Living God, Leon Morris (IVP 1960)